NANA'S *Notes*

A Parenting Primer

The Manual For Every New Baby!

by

Cindy "Nana" Parente

NANA'S
Notes

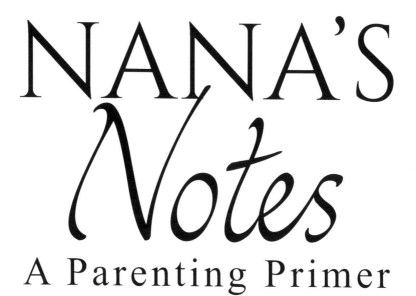

NANA'S *Notes*
A Parenting Primer

The Manual For Every New Baby!

by

Cindy "Nana" Parente

Nana Approved, LLC
Merrimack, New Hampshire, USA

WARNING: Adult supervision is required.
Playful activities can be unintentionally dangerous.
Babies are extremely fragile. Use extreme care.

Dear Reader,

I hesitated to bring this forward because I'm only a "Nana". But then I remembered a Dad, a partner in a prestigious regional law firm, who had come to check us out. When I demonstrated the activity – how to hold his son and what to do – he asked, "Why?" Once I explained this helps both sides of the brain work together, he was excited to participate. Then I remember the many thousands more, the Moms, Dads, Grandparents, Aunties, Uncles (on both sides!) and I knew I had to try.

My only hope is that I have been able to convey through the written word that which I was able to give in person.

Kind regards,
Nana

PRAISE FOR NANA'S NOTES

Kristina B., Pediatric DPT, Mom

Thanks for this! It looks great and is very informative without being too overwhelming for new parents. I loved the part about exposing babies to different types of music. This was something I was actually wondering about this week, if it should only be "baby" songs, but sounds like a nice variety can be good (and keep the adults from going crazy listening to "Twinkle Twinkle" all day every day).

I do really like how your activities are simple and easy to implement but give nice direction. Even as someone with a background in infant development it's overwhelming trying to figure out what exactly to do so having a few straightforward activities like these are great!

We started doing some baby signs a couple of months ago and it's amazing to see him catching on.

Kim P., RDN, Mom

I loved it! It gave me some great ideas for activities we could do together. It also gave me peace of mind that what I am doing is helping her learn and grow. I love the "voice" or "tone" of it. I read it like you were speaking to me! Haha! Thanks again for sharing your expertise and fun ideas with me.

Betty M., PhD, Educational Leadership K-12, Mom

Sign language has such incredible value. Many times, it clarifies what a child can't express verbally, for whatever reason. One time when I was teaching Kindergarten, a child's family member came in and taught us sign language. At the end of the year, I was testing this child's letter sound knowledge. I made a "K" sound and asked her to point to that letter in the alphabet on the wall. She couldn't do it, so I assumed she didn't know the letter. Then she suddenly signed it for me! It turned out she had dyslexia and needed glasses, which is why she couldn't see the letters properly on the wall. When she signed that letter, we knew something was going on with her eyes!

Your Nana's Notes are filled with wonderful activities! And I think it's great you have added the physical areas each activity addresses.

CONTENTS

INTRODUCTION

Congratulations and welcome to parenthood!

Exciting? Yes! Frightening? Yes! Overwhelming? You bet! But rest assured, your capacity to love, nurture, and protect your baby comes from the deepest, most ancient region of your brain and will only grow. Your baby's capacity to love and trust you stems from the exact same region so one could say, you're made for each other!

You have given birth to a brilliant individual with almost limitless potential. As the primary memory maker, your job is tremendous. Your baby will learn *everything* from you: how to listen, how to learn, how to love. Love travels through centuries, through our families.

At birth, most of your baby's sensory systems are fully developed and functioning (sight will catch up soon). Information gathered through our senses (touch, smell, sound, taste, sight, body awareness and pull of gravity) is known as sensory integration. Sensory integration is a primary source of learning, indeed a very pillar upon which all future learning will be formed.

Playful, meaningful experiences enhance sensory integration. Play is how we learn. Being playful with your baby will serve you well for a lifetime. Through playful interactions you both grow, your baby builds trust and benefits from all the appropriate stimulation and you, through observations, will come to understand how your baby learns best.

The activities outlined in this parenting primer are designed as a steppingstone, if you will, in understanding your child's developmental progression and how you can best help. You will fill your days with song, dance, play and so much more and I promise, you will not believe how quickly time can pass!

CHAPTER 1

Glossary & Other Things Nana Wants You to Know

Nana's Notes: *Intended to give you an overview of our sensory systems, I have placed this front and center because understanding this is the "WHY" behind all the activities to follow. The sensory systems appear in sequence of in utero development and are highlighted next to each activity. I've scattered the terms he, she, his, hers, him, and her indiscriminately throughout.*

Tactile: Tactile refers to touch. It is the first sensory system to develop in utero.

> ✓ **Discriminative** touch, known for its protective qualities, allows us to feel and localize a light touch on the surface like a tickle or an itch, to feel pressure beneath the surface, to alert us to pain and sudden temperature changes. It plays a role in our ability to recognize the shape, texture and function of objects. Food choices are impacted by tactile input. Serious consider-

ation must be given when selecting products and fabrics that touch your baby's skin.

- ✓ **Affective** touch, known for its caressing qualities of gentle stroking, is the emotional component. Through your touch, your baby will learn about love.
- ✓ **Intentional** touch is a combination of both discriminative and affective touch and is explored more thoroughly in Chapter 4, *Massaging Baby.*

Auditory: *Auditory* refers to our ability to hear. This system becomes functional at about 25 weeks in utero. By birth, your baby can distinguish Mom's voice and within days, Dad's voice as well. Knowing babies are stimulated by higher-pitched sounds, we all adopt the high-pitched, melodic "baby speak" to accommodate.

Your baby's auditory system needs outside stimulation during the crucial first few months to develop properly. By repeating favorite songs and providing meaningful speech, you are enabling your child to make the connections for the sounds of your language. Avoid loud, startling sounds but do offer a variety of "sound makers," such as musical egg shakes. Ring some high-pitched chimes. As your baby's vision matures these "tools" will help create the neural pathways for hearing and sound localization.

Vestibular: *Vestibular* refers to the balance system. Located in the inner ear it begins functioning about halfway through pregnancy. It is the center for motor control and is crucial for body and head orientation, coordination, motion detection and eye control. It allows babies to detect motion, to feel secure in movement and to recognize the pull of gravity.

Proprioception: This refers to the position of the body and joint movements. It keeps track of our limbs and controls muscle stretch and contraction. Development of this system is crucial for spatial orientation and posture as well as muscle strength and tone. It was once described to me as that sense you get when someone has readjusted your car seat. You know your surroundings have changed because your body feels different.

Vision: The sense that takes the longest to develop is often regarded as the "master" sense. Approximately 80 percent of all learning is facilitated through vision. When you consider vision is the sense through which color and light are received you have the ingredients for wonder to develop!

The first week after birth, your baby will recognize your face within a distance of only eight to twelve inches. Within a month he will try to mimic your facial expressions. By two months vision has expanded to about 18 inches and some details are beginning to emerge. Motion stimulates visual awareness and your baby will track items with his whole head until around three months of age when you will notice eyes-only tracking begins. Color recognition begins to emerge around four months of age. This is also about the time he will find his hand and spend hours examining it. Both eyes begin to work together around five months of age. This is when depth perception, our ability to see the world in three dimensions, begins to take focus. Reaching for objects while following his hand is the beginning of depth perception. It will take a few years for depth perception to be fully developed and integrated into motion with ease.

Crossing the Midline: The midline is an imaginary line straight down the middle of our body. Crossing the midline indicates both sides of the brain are communicating together. This is observed in clapping hands and rolling over. Crossing the midline is necessary for crawling, reading, writing and drawing. Encourage reaching across the midline whenever possible. Begin by maintaining eye contact and gently swaying your baby in front of you, to one side and then the other, always coming back to center for a pause. While your baby is laying on his back, slowly move an object from side to side. Once your baby can sit on his own, place objects slightly out of reach and encourage reaching with the opposite hand to retrieve them.

Reaching, Grasping, Gripping and Releasing (RGGR): At birth, your baby's hand will be clenched in a tight fist, a vestige of life in utero. Early, intentional reaching depends on visual connections between an object and your baby's hand. Although the motion is "jerky" at first, smooth reaching and grasping generally occurs around six months of age. Babies begin with the "pincer grasp" utilizing only the pointer finger and thumb. Use caution as they can get their fingers stuck in small holes. Being able to grasp and release objects is the first step towards self-care like self-feeding. All fine motor skills begin with reaching, grasping, gripping and releasing. A strong grip is usually a sign of good health. By employing our opposable thumbs while gripping we are contracting the muscles in our arms that protect our joints. ***Never grab your child by the wrist.***

Taste and Smell: Although not specifically addressed here, both senses are needed for survival and are quite mature at birth. Research suggests an infant can sense Mom by her scent before she hears her. At birth, your baby's mouth is literally covered with taste buds and most babies do prefer sweet tastes above all else. Your baby will start putting everything in her mouth, as part of her discovery process, as soon as she discovers her hands. That probably won't stop until approximately 16 months of age when she begins to explore objects for function and use rather than shape and form.

Cognitive Skills: This refers to the building of learning skills, the core skills our brain uses to think, learn, remember, reason, imagine, and to pay attention. Fun, structured, meaningful sensory integrative activities, like those outlined in this manual, facilitate everything coming together.

Trust: Trust develops in stages, beginning at birth. The first stage develops when a baby cries and her needs are met by a loving adult. This is a time of deep bonding, when promises of a lifetime are silently made.

The second stage is about trusting the environment and the routines of daily life. It's about bringing order to their lives, knowing their home is their home, day follows night. This is also a time of great exploration and having a trusted hand nearby, offering guidance, helps deepen self-confidence. Self-confidence is necessary to develop the final stage of trust – the ability to trust oneself – knowing how to act, be patient, to apply skills and imagination to tasks. The stages of trust build upon each other and these transitions are not smooth and steady. Everyone takes life at their own pace. There are those who jump into a pool with two feet and others who inch their way in. Work with *your* child. Trust *your* child is telling you the truth. Try not to measure one child against another but rather, read your child's body language, listen not only with your ears but with your heart and always let them know how deeply they are wanted.

Toys/Tools: Toys *are* tools for babies. Throughout this Primer, I refer to four very basic "tools" chosen for their durability, versatility and accessibility: beach balls, bean bags, musical shakers and juggling scarves. The function of these tools changes as your child's development progresses and you will use them creatively for years.

CHAPTER 2

Tummy Time Activities

Nana's Notes: *Tummy time is an important building block that starts with you – your chest, your legs, the amount of time you spend on your tummy face to face with your baby, the amount of time you spend holding your baby tummy down as you walk around. Spending time on their tummies helps develop and strengthen the muscles in their hands, arms, shoulders, and neck. Tummy time also helps to strengthen their depth perception. It is hard work and your baby may fuss but, the following activities are designed to help. Always remember, back to sleep, tummy to play!*

- Place your newborn on your chest. Skin-to-skin is best. Gradually lower your back until you are laying down on your back. Be sure to keep one hand on your baby's back for reassurance. ***(Trust, vestibular and tactile stimulation)***

- Place a clean sheet on the floor and gently place your baby on his tummy. Do not use pillows or anything soft. Stretch out on your tummy to meet face to face. Entertain him with songs and stories. Roll over onto your back and let your baby see you upside down. *(Upper body strength, facial recognition, proprioceptive and vestibular stimulation, vertical vision)*

- Carry your baby, face down, on your forearm. Place your baby against your chest, facing outward. Place your arm across your baby's body so that his head rests in the crook of your elbow. As you roll your baby onto your arm, place your other hand securely on your baby's back. Walk and dance around to your favorite tunes. Personally, I've always loved a slowed down version of Michael Jackson's "Rock With You" to calm a baby. *(Proprioceptive and vestibular stimulation, balance, rhythm, depth perception)*

- Place your baby on his tummy on the floor. Using musical egg shakers, gently tap out a beat on one side, then the other. Bean bags work well, too. *(Sound localization)*

Nana's Notes: *Do not use maracas. The shape of the handle might pose a choking hazard.*

- Slowly raise and lower a bean bag in front of your baby so she can visually track the object up and down. *(Vertical vision)*

- Lie on your back and place your baby on your shins. Holding by the torso, gently lift and lower your legs. I love singing "Let's Go Fly a Kite" from the movie *Mary Poppins* during this activity. *(Depth perception, rhythm, trust)*

Blanket Roll

- Roll up a blanket or use a sleeping bag. Place your baby on her tummy lengthwise along the roll. Spot carefully by holding her by the torso, gently roll side to side. *(Proprioceptive and vestibular stimulation, pull of gravity, upper body strength*)

- Place your baby on her back, lengthwise, spot carefully and gently roll side to side while maintaining eye contact. *(Crossing the midline, visual tracking, vestibular stimulation)*

- Once your baby can easily raise her arms over her head, place your baby across the roll on the tummy and gently roll back and forth. Spot carefully. *(Depth perception, vestibular stimulation)*

- Place small objects like the musical egg shakers or bean bags in front of your baby and encourage reaching and grasping while you gently roll her back and forth. *(Vestibular, depth perception, eye/hand coordination)*

- Now, just for fun, place your baby on her back across the roll. Holding by the torso, gently roll her away and then give her an extra kiss when you roll her back to you. *(Trust, vestibular stimulation)*

For the Almost to Just Crawler

Nana's Notes: *Tummy time is the precursor to crawling. I know it's hard to imagine your infant ever crawling, however, the dash between "almost" and "just" is a mere flash in time. They have been working so hard towards this, absorbing their body weight in their hands, pushing up, reaching, crossing the midline, developing their eye/hand coordination, depth perception and vertical vision. Together you have stimulated their proprioceptive awareness, stimulated their balance system and supported their upper and lower body strength development. Lower body strength is essential for motion. Careful spotting is needed while they try to get into a crawling position. You can kneel behind them, placing their knees in the appropriate position while absorbing their body weight.*

- Place your baby on a blanket with objects scattered just out of reach. Encourage reaching by tapping the toy. **Multiple sensory input may be needed** such as gently stroking the top of your baby's hand followed by tapping the toy to encourage reaching. *(**Reaching, depth perception, proprioceptive stimulation, neck and upper body strength, vertical vision stimulation**)*

- Once stable on all fours, they will test their balance by rocking back and forth all the time, even to the point it may wake them during the night! This will occur again when they are getting ready to walk. *(**Vestibular stimulation, upper body strength, vertical vision, proprioceptive stimulation**)*

- Once they are secure on their knees, to encourage crawling, place your hand on the bottom of their feet to be a wedge they can push off from. *(**Tactile stimulation**)*

- Once your baby begins crawling, encourage crawling with a bean bag or musical egg shaker in hand. This helps develop the curvature of the hand. *(RGGR, muscular development, pro-proprioceptive awareness, depth perception)*

Nana's Notes: *Slides and ramps become powerful tools at this time. The greater the angle, the faster the slide. Slides help develop both upper and lower body strength, offer vestibular stimulation, stimulate understanding of the pull of gravity, challenge the proprioceptive system, stimulate depth perception and are plain old fun.*

- Place your baby at the bottom of the slide or ramp, on his knees. Place your hands on the bottom of his feet to create a ledge he can push from. Follow in this manner up to the top and gently pull him back to the bottom. **(Lower body strength, reaching, pull of gravity, depth perception, proprioceptive stimulation, vertical vision)**

Nana's Notes: *Do not place your hand on your baby's bottom while he is trying to climb up a ramp or slide. Once he senses your hand there, he gives up trying. By keeping your hand on his feet, you encourage your baby to do the actual work needed.*

> ONCE HE SENSES YOUR HAND THERE, HE GIVES UP TRYING.

- Place your baby at the top of the slide, on her knees, facing toward the bottom. Spot carefully by holding the torso. Encourage her to crawl down to the bottom. *(Upper body strength, depth perception, pull of gravity, proprioceptive stimulation.)*

- Place your baby on her tummy at the top of the slide, feet towards the bottom. Go for a slide-ride. Be sure to vary the speed! *(Fun)*

Nana's Notes: *An independent seated slide usually occurs right around the time your baby begins to walk. As your baby becomes a competent sitter, it's time to try a seated slide on a gentle angle. A seated slide requires us to shift our center of gravity by leaning forward ever so slightly. To facilitate, place yourself at the bottom. You may need to offer a finger for him to grip to encourage him to lean forward. Never push from behind. If using an outdoor slide, always make sure the slide surface is an appropriate temperature.*

> A SEATED SLIDE REQUIRES US TO SHIFT OUR CENTER OF GRAVITY BY LEANING FORWARD EVER SO SLIGHTLY.

CHAPTER 3

Music: Another Way to Play

"Music expresses that which cannot be put into words and that which cannot remain silent."
– Victor Hugo

Nana's Notes: *Music is a universal language that has provoked deep emotional responses across all cultures since ancient times. Research confirms what families have known forever - babies who are rocked, cradled, and sung to thrive. In fact, board-certified music therapists are introducing music in NICUs (neonatal intensive care units) worldwide with positive results being reported. (Visit MusicTherapy.org for more info)*

Beat perception actually begins in the womb. Rocking your little one or gently walking about while singing familiar lullabies has an extraordinarily calming effect. It lifts your baby's mood, while simultaneously relieving stress and lowering heart rate.

Your voice is the most beautiful sound in the world to your baby and singing is a natural way to bond and communicate. You may have to sing an octave or two higher than usual as higher notes stimulate brain

activity. Your face changes ever so slight-
ly as you sing so watching you is a huge
treat that will delight your baby all day.
Repeating favorite songs helps develop
listening and cognitive skills needed to
learn language. In time your baby will
come to anticipate the next verse and will
feel pride when they are right! When you

> REPEATING FAVORITE
> SONGS HELPS DEVELOP
> LISTENING AND
> COGNITIVE SKILLS
> NEEDED TO LEARN
> LANGUAGE

copy your baby's sounds, you strengthen communication skills like, "your
turn, my turn." The "Fa-la-la-la-la" part of "Deck the Halls" is perfect
for this.

Music is created and celebrated worldwide, reflecting each cul-
ture's past and present. In each culture, lullabies and dance are present
and handed down generation to generation.

There are numerous musical genres that are widely recognized:
classical, jazz, rock, blues, to name a few and each genre can be subdi-
vided. It's impossible to separate movement from music and each genre
will inspire you to move differently. By dancing uninhibitedly with your
child, you are encouraging listening and deeper cognitive skills as well
as the freedom to develop their own movement signature. Try to expose
your baby to as many different musical genres as possible as you may
be surprised by which one touches his soul.

There is abundant research regarding music and spatial intelli-
gence. Music helps develop the ability to see patterns in space and time.
Think chess, architecture, athletes running down a field timing their
movements to meet a ball. I refer you to the Bulletin of the Council
for Research in Music Education *(full citation at the end) for further*
information.

All of your childhood favorites will become your child's favorites and
all the old love songs will take on new meaning. "Baby, I'm Yours" by
Barbara Lewis and "Simply Irresistible" by Robert Palmer come to mind.

Musical Activities

Lullabies: Rocking and swaying to lullabies is timeless. While listening to recorded lullabies is good, singing lullabies is magical. In our family we have a top-ten all-time favorites list ranging from Brahms to the Beatles! I know we've changed the words to some and improvised on others, but the desired effect was achieved, peaceful sleep for our little ones.

Nana's Notes: *Music can be used to promote body awareness, from "Wake Up Toes" to "The Hokey Pokey," to encourage language development, trust and listening skills. Always stay within the movement comfort level of your baby. Never force a joint movement and never toss your baby up in the air.*

To the tune of "Clap, Clap, Clap Your Hands," try:

Clapping	Rolling
Tapping	Kicking
Rocking	Shrugging
Swaying	Blinking
Twisting	

- Sing "Head, Shoulders, Knees and Toes" while touching your baby's body.

- Do "The Hokey-Pokey" in front of a mirror.

- Use a beach ball as a percussion instrument. While your baby is touching the ball, gently tap out the beat to a favorite song. **(Tactile, visual, auditory stimulation, rhythm)**

For the Competent Sitter

Add lap rides. Place your baby on your lap, facing you to begin, facing outward as they get stronger. Spot carefully by holding your baby's torso. Gently bounce your legs to the steady beat. Remember, the beat goes on even during the silent times. Try alternating your legs and marching your legs up and down for a greater balance challenge. *(Vestibular and proprioceptive stimulation, rhythm)*

To encourage rhythm, offer your baby two musical egg shakers, one for each hand.

- Shake them in time to the beat.
- Tap them to the beat.
- Clap them to the beat.
- Tap double time.
- Raise them high.

Nana's Notes: *I named my daughter Alexandra without giving a thought to a little girl trying to learn how to spell such a name! Singing it to the tune of the British National Anthem saved the day. It went like this:*

Alexandra, Alexandra all the way.

A- L- E -X-A- N- D- R- A!

Try to add music, song and dance, to your everyday activities. Sing "Rub-a-dub-dub" during bath time. Create a marching band. Do a polka. Let music help you act out stories. Music can lighten a mood and bring people of all ages and cultures together. If we listen, we will hear music everywhere!

CHAPTER 4

Massaging Baby

Nana's Notes: *Massage is another ancient, cross-cultural phenomenon offering extensive health benefits for infants as well as adults. Some of these benefits include; boosting the immune system, improving circulation, relieving stress, promoting better sleep and bonding. I was trained in two massage concepts; the Indian concept of balancing and releasing energy, and the muscle-toning Swedish massage which promotes good circulation. Worldwide, we are taught that touch is the language of love.*

I recommend waiting a week or so after you get home before beginning a massage. Massaging your baby should be an enjoyable experience for both of you. Your touch should be intentional, neither a tickle nor a deep tissue massage. Make sure your baby is neither hungry nor just fed, alert and not sleepy. You will want to "set the mood" by playing some soft, soothing music in the background. If it's chilly, only remove the articles of clothing for the area you will be massaging. Before beginning, warm the massage oil be-

> MASSAGING YOUR BABY SHOULD BE AN ENJOYABLE EXPERIENCE FOR BOTH OF YOU.

tween your palms. (I like grapeseed oil as it is plant-based and available at your local grocery store.)

Take a few cleansing breaths, remember your love for your baby and, when you are calm, ask your baby permission. It is respectful.

When the massage session is done, gently pick up your child and rock together for a few minutes. This kind of closeness is magical.

Massage Techniques

Nana's Notes: *Start with massaging your baby's legs as they are used to getting their diapers changed by now. Don't rush things as it won't be long until you are giving your baby a full body massage every day.*

Legs and feet: Spread the warmed oil down your baby's leg. At all times, be very careful of the knee joint. Starting at the thigh, use a gentle milking motion (gently squeezing and releasing), all the way down to the ankle. And then back up again. Repeat several times. Next, starting at the thigh again, use a gentle twisting motion to massage across the muscles all the way down to the ankle and back again. Repeat several times. At the ankle, massage in gentle circular motions. Take your baby's foot into your hand and gently rub your thumb from the heel to the toe, one thumb after the other. Gently straighten each toe. Place your forefinger under the toes and gently rotate. Massage with circular motions in the arch of the foot and ankle. Place your hands on your baby's thigh and "swoosh" all the way down, in one motion, to the toes for a final release of tension. Repeat on the other leg.

Tummy: Always check that your baby's bottom is flat on the floor. After warming the oil, place your hands under the breastbone and slowly "paddle" one hand after the other, straight down. Repeat several times. Gently place your left forearm across your baby's hip area. Using two fingers of your right hand, draw a semi-circle from your elbow to your wrist, always ending with a downward motion on your baby's left side to aid with digestion. If your baby is suffering gas pains, try massaging the arch of the foot in a circular motion. It helps!

Chest: After warming the oil, place your hands on your baby's chest. Gently stroke outward towards the sides, following the rib cage, like opening a book. Next, create a heart shape. Beginning at the bottom of your baby's breastbone, using two fingers in an upward motion towards the shoulders and then down the sides to a point below the rib cage. Next, create a butterfly pattern. Starting at the right hip, stroke upwards diagonally across the body to the left shoulder. Repeat by starting at the left hip and stroking diagonally towards the right shoulder. Repeat in a rhythmic pattern. When complete, place your hands on your baby's shoulders and "swoosh" all the way to the toes.

Arms: Meet your baby where they are developmentally. If they are not ready to un-hug themselves, simply massage the outer part of the arm. For those infants who are willing to let their arms move away from their torso, massaging the arms is very similar to massaging the legs. Starting at the shoulder, begin a gentle "milking" motion, a gentle squeeze and release all the way down to the wrist and back up again. This is followed by a gently "twisting" motion across the muscles. Use extra care when near the elbow. Massage the wrist using small circular motions. Gently open your baby's hand and straighten each finger remembering to only follow the range of motion your baby determines. Using your thumbs, gently massage the palm of the hand downward towards the fingertips. Likewise, on the top of the hand from the wrist to the fingertips. When done, "swoosh" in one motion from the shoulder to the fingers.

Nana's Notes: *Be very gently when massaging the face. Much of our identity is associated with our face. You must always tell them they are beautiful in every way.*

Face: Use your thumbs to gently swipe across the brow, starting at the bridge of the nose and sweeping outward towards the temples. Next, gently swipe under the eyes to relax the sinus passages. Next use your thumbs to gently outline a smile around the lips. Finally, stroke behind the ears, along the jawline and under the chin.

Back: Sitting with your back supported and your legs extended, place your baby across your lap, tummy down. Rest your hands across the shoulders then gently move across the back muscles from the shoulders to the tailbone. Using your fingertips, work down along the spine and gently massage the muscles around the rib cage towards the side. Starting at the tailbone, make gentle circular motions up alongside your baby's spine. To end, rest one hand on the baby's bottom. Using the palm of your other hand, stroke down the back to meet your stable hand. When done, spread your fingers and sweep all the way down the back.

CHAPTER 5

Play, Play, Play & Then Play Some More!

"Play is the work of childhood." – *Fred Rogers*

Nana's Notes: *The Convention on the Rights of the Child, adopted by the General Assembly of the United Nations in Nov. 1989 states: "Every child has a right to rest and leisure, to engage in play and recreational activities that are age appropriate to the child, and participation in cultural and artistic activities."*

> I THINK YOUNG CHILDREN RARELY GET AS MUCH PLAY AS THEIR BRAINS NEED IN THIS COUNTRY...

The importance of play cannot be overstated. Dr. Jaak Panskepp, a renowned neuroscientist and psycho-biologist said, "I think young children rarely get as much play as their brains need in this country... We have to develop a society that understands play and the many good things it does for the children's brains and minds."

Play Ball!

Nana's Notes: *Balls are used in almost every sport and game we play. Used to roll, throw, catch, kick, bounce, hit, and pass, used either individually or with a team, balls come in many sizes and shapes. Perfect for infants, we begin with beach balls, available everywhere! They are colorful, lightweight, slow moving and large enough to give your baby an opportunity to track and grasp. I recommend them for parties instead of balloons.*

- Place your baby on his back in front of you. Inflate and deflate the beach ball several times. Let him feel the cool breeze as it deflates. *(Auditory, visual and tactile stimulation)*

- Raise the beach ball to your shoulder level and begin to gently twirl the ball. *(Visual stimulation)*

- While your baby is focused on the twirling ball, slowly move it to the right, back to center and then to the left and back to center. *(Crossing the midline, visual stimulation)*

- Bring the ball back to center and slowly raise the ball up towards the top of her head, now back down again. *(Vertical vision)*

- With your baby on her back, toss the ball up in the air. *(Visual tracking, depth perception)*

- Beginning at your baby's toes, slowly roll the ball up your baby's body and back down again. You can chant, "A line going up, a line going down, a line going up and up, a line going down." *(Tactile and auditory stimulation)*

- With your baby on your lap facing outward, have someone roll the ball to you and then roll it back. Chant, "I roll the ball to you, you roll the ball to me, I roll the ball to you and then roll it back to me." Once your baby is a competent sitter, you can play "catch" together in this way. *(Visual tracking, depth perception, auditory stimulation)*

- Either sitting or lying down, place your baby's hands on the ball. Using it as a percussion instrument, gently tap the ball and let your baby feel the vibrations. *(Tactile and auditory stimulation)*

- Bounce the ball. *(Visual and auditory stimulation)*

- Baby Soccer is played with two adults, standing, facing each other. Firmly grasp your baby by the torso *(not under the armpits!),* from behind. Begin by gently swinging your baby between your legs. Once he's comfortable, have the opposing adult roll the beach ball to you. Swing again and score! *(Visual tracking, depth perception, vestibular and proprioceptive stimulation)*

- Place the beachball in the middle of a small colorful sheet. With 2 adults holding the edges, gently shake the sheet up and down. Baby can be in your lap or even on the sheet with the beachball! *(Visual, tactile, auditory, vestibular stimulation)*

Bean Bag Activities

Nana's Notes: *Bean bags also come in a variety of shapes and weights. They offer a nice contrast to the lightweight beach balls and are often easier to manipulate than a ball. Bean bags stay where they land thus offering a child the opportunity to explore gravity. Guaranteed to be a long-lasting favorite, this versatile tool will be used extensively as your child masters concept development, imaginary play, and pre-sport skills. You want a high quality, durable bean bag as your baby will inevitably use this as a teething tool, as well. As always, be cautious of the choking hazard all teething toys present.*

- Place your baby on her back. Show her the bean bag as you gently "crumple" it so she can hear the sound. *(Visual and auditory stimulation)*

- Raise the bean bag so she can see it then slowly move the bean bag to the left, back to center, move it to the right and back to center, moving slowly so she can visually track it. *(Cross the midline, visual stimulation)*

- Crumple the bean bag to one side, out of sight. *(Sound localization)*

- Place the bean bag on your head, gently tip your head and catch the bean bag in your hand. *(Visual stimulation)*

- As your baby becomes mobile, offer the bean bag to hold while crawling. This helps with the curvature of the hand. *(Tactile and proprioceptive stimulation)*

Scarf Play

Nana's Notes: *Juggling scarves offer the perfect, whimsical floating object, allowing for optimal tracking, reaching and grasping. They also add color and excitement to dances.*

Use only with adult supervision and always store safely away from your baby

- Peek-a-boo. Place your baby on his back so he can see you. Place the see-through scarf on *your* head. Chant, "Everyone loves peek-a-boo, peek-a-boo, peek-a-boo, everyone loves peek-a-boo, peek-a-boo with you." *(Visual and auditory stimulation, RGGR, rhythm)*

- Roll the scarf into a ball in your hands, slowly open your hands for a "Blooming Flower". *(Visual stimulation)*

- Place your baby on her back and wave the scarf up and down, side to side. *(Visual tracking, tactile stimulation)*

- Crumple the scarf into a ball in your hands and then toss it into the air so it can float down. *(Visual tracking)*

- Use it as a prop while dancing. *(Visual stimulation)*

CHAPTER 6

Introducing Sign Language to Babies

Nana's Notes: *Sign language is as varied as all spoken languages yet the benefits are universal. Introducing sign language to your infant has shown increased cognitive and emotional development. I refer you to* "The Long-Term Impact of Symbolic Gesturing During Infancy" *by Linda P. Acredolo and Susan W. Goodwyn for in-depth details (full citation at the end).*

Here are some ASL signs to help you communicate with your non-verbal child. Always remember to use the word associated with the sign. In no time your family will create signs of your own.

"I'm hungry."
"Do you want to eat?"

Pinch the fingertips of one hand together. Move your hand towards your mouth.

"I'm tired!"
"Do you want to take a nap?"

Place the palm of your hand against your cheek and lean into it a bit.

"More, please."
"Would you like some more?"

Pinching your fingertips together on both hands, move your hands together so that your fingertips meet in the middle.

"Thank you."

Place your fingertips on your chin. Gesture your hand outward.

"Please."

Make a soft fist. Place your fist on your chest and make circular motions.

"I love you."

Raise your pinky and index fingers while extending your thumb.

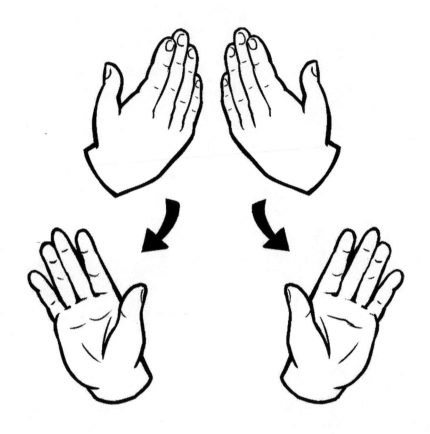

"All done"

Place your hands facing your shoulders. In a sweeping motion, turn your hands so your palms are facing out.

CHAPTER 7

Final Thoughts

Nana's Notes: I am sincerely happy for you. Those promises you made in the silence of the night; to always love, to always protect, to always be there no matter what, are for life. You will be offered advice from everyone about everything, you will be judged about your parenting skills for the rest of your life but, none of that matters. Follow your heart. Your job is to create a home where your baby can flourish. The goal is to raise someone who believes in himself, someone who is capable of giving and receiving love, someone brave enough to ultimately follow their own dreams. I believe in you.

WORKS CITED

Acredolo, Linda P. and Goodwyn, Susan W. "The Long-Term Impact of Symbolic Gesturing During Infancy." Paper presented at the International Conference on Infant Studies (July 18, 2000: Brighton, UK).

Rauscher, Frances H. "Music Exposure and the Development of Spatial Intelligence in Children." Bulletin of the Council for Research in Music Education, *No. 142, 1999, pp. 35–47. JSTOR, www.jstor.org/ stable/40319006. Accessed 4 Aug. 2020.*

ACKNOWLEDGMENTS

I want to thank everybody starting with my parents, my sister, my sweet Grandmamma. To all my childhood friends, it was so fun growing up together. To every teacher who took the time to reach me, to teach me. To the many thousands of families who allowed me into their lives during their most precious moments. To my children and grandchildren who continue to teach me everything I need to know. To everyone who helped me get this project off the ground; Lacey, Michelle, Betty, Angela, Carol, Susie, Ann Marie, Kristina, Kim, Bryan, Stacy, Praise and Allison, I would have been lost without you! And finally, to my Michael, the original Pied Piper, I will follow you anywhere, anytime.

ABOUT THE AUTHOR

Nana was born, raised and educated in NYC. Upon finishing school, she marched down to Wall Street where she was fast-tracked between NYC and London. *THEN SHE HAD A BABY!!* She completely embraced a shift in direction and moved with her family to what she calls, "Sleepy Town, NH". For the next few decades, she owned and operated the world's premier "franchised" and "certified" Early Childhood Development Programs. She came to look at herself as everyone's Grandmother, often saying, "They come, they play, they go home with Mommy." When her young cousin was expecting, Nana looked through the gift registry and came away knowing she had greater gifts to give. She sat down and began writing that very day. It is the insights of having personally worked with literally thousands of families that she brings to these pages.

Moms get their best information from other Moms.
If you connected with this book, please help me
reach other Moms by leaving a review on Amazon.

Ways to stay in touch!

Like us on Facebook

Sign up for our Newsletter

Filled with relevant news, research and topics of interest,
I promise to only reach out when there's news to share.
Plus, you'll be among the first to know of new releases!

Your information will be kept private and you can
unsubscribe at any time.

Be sure to visit our Publishers website frequently!

NanaApproved.com

Only the beginning...

coming soon

Nana's Notes: *Who ever coined the phrase "school of hard knocks" must have had this segment of the population in mind. The sheer grit and determination exhibited by these little tykes is awe inspiring.*

Mommy's Notes

Daddy's Notes

Made in the USA
Middletown, DE
01 April 2023

27463270R00029